AFRICAN SMALL PUBLISHERS' CATALOGUE 2018

EDITED AND COMPILED BY
COLLEEN HIGGS

African Small Publishers' Catalogue 2018

First published by Modjaji Books 2018

www.modjajibooks.co.za
info@modjajibooks.co.za

Individual listings and adverts @ the contributors. All other text © Modjaji Books.

Editor: Colleen Higgs
Cover image: Toni Olivier
Production: Electric Book Works

ISBN (Print): 978-1-928215-72-1
ISBN (Digital download): 978-1-928215-73-8

Contents

Introduction

This is the fourth edition of the *African Small Publishers' Catalogue*. Once again we have many more publishers and some of the publishers we featured last time have either left the scene, or their circumstances have changed such that they don't want to be in the catalogue. The catalogue is a showcase of the variety and extent of independent and small publishing in Africa. It is still weighted with many more South African publishers, but each time we have brought out a new edition, there are more listings from a wider spread of African publishers. The catalogue aims to uncover and highlight the work and existence of small publishers in Africa. I hope that librarians, booksellers, books' page editors, educators, readers, writers and bigger publishers will be enriched by having access to these publishers and that the publishers themselves will find new customers, access to funds and technologies that will enable them to thrive. It is thrilling to see all the writers and publishers who are toiling away, doing extraordinary creative cultural work.

The editor

Colleen Higgs is a publisher who also writes poetry and short fiction. She has had two poetry collections published: *Halfborn Woman* (2004), *Lava Lamp Poems* (2011) and a collection of short stories: *Looking for Trouble* (2012). She started Modjaji Books in 2007, it has since become an internationally recognized feminist press. Many Modjaji titles have won awards or been short listed. Modjaji Books is a member of the International Alliance of Independent Publishers. Higgs is a publishing activist, and this catalogue is one of the ways she contributes to book development and raising the profile of independent publishing in Africa. She lives in Cape Town with her daughter, two dogs and a cat.

Listings

Aerial Publishing

SOUTH AFRICA

Postal Address   Grahamstown

PO Box 6082

Grahamstown

6140

Email   aerial.publishing.grahamstown@gmail.com

Phone   +27 046 622 5081

Aerial Publishing is a Grahamstown-based community publisher, publishing mainly previously unpublished Eastern Cape poets. It emerged from the popular four month creative writing course which has been running at the Rhodes Institute for the Study of English in Africa (ISEA) since 1998, when writers associated with the course decided to publish individual collections. As new writers are published, they are invited to become part of the collective which selects, edits and publishes the next books. All money made from sales goes towards the publishing of future titles. Aerial Publishing's first two poetry collections were published in 2004 and we're still going strong.

aerial publishing

African Minds

Physical address	4 Eccleston Place
	Somerset West
	Cape Town
	7130
Website	www.africanminds.org.za
Email	info@africanminds.co.za
Phone	+27 21 852 7093
Twitter	African_Minds
Contacts	François van Schalkwyk

African Minds is an open access, not-for-profit publisher. African Minds publishes predominantly in the social sciences and its authors are typically African researchers or those who share a close affinity with the continent. African Minds offers innovative approaches to those frustrated by a lack of support from traditional publishers or by their anachronistic approach to making research available. At African Minds, the emphasis is less on the commercial viability of publications than on fostering access, openness and debate in the pursuit of growing and deepening the African knowledge base.

African Sun Press

Postal Address	PO Box 16415
	Vlaeberg
	Cape Town
	8018
Website	www.afsun.co.za
Email	afpress@iafrica.com
Phone	+27 21 461 1601
Contacts	Patricia Schonstein

We are South Africa's leading poetry anthologists, publishing the *Africa! Anthologies*; the *McGregor Poetry Festival Anthologies*; and *Stanzas* – a quarterly for new poems. We administer the rights of Patricia Schonstein and Don Pinnock and curate the Pinnock Photographic Archive.

African Sun Press
www.afsun.co.za

Patricia Schonstein is a novelist and poet. Her work is endorsed by Nobel Laureates JM Coetzee and Archbishop Tutu.

Don Pinnock is a former editor of *Getaway*; author of natural history and travel; renowned criminologist; expert on youth-at-risk.

Douglas Reid Skinner is a former editor of *New Contrast* (1988–1992). His poetry is published in five volumes and two books of translations.

AmaBooks

Postal Address	PO Box AC 1066
	Ascot
	Bulawayo
Website	www.amabooksbyo.com
Email	amabooksbyo@gmail.com
Phone	+26 3 9 246602
Contacts	Jane Morris

'amaBooks

amaBooks is a small, independent publisher based in Zimbabwe's second city Bulawayo. We publish novels, short stories, poetry, with a few local history and culture titles. Our main focus is Zimbabwean literary fiction in English, work that reflects contemporary life in the country. Since our inception we have been able to give a platform to many emerging writers, as well as those who are more established. Over 200 writers have now been published by amaBooks. Several of our titles have acheived recognition both nationally and internationally, including those by Tendai Huchu, Bryony Rheam, Togara Muzanenhamo, John Eppel, Christopher Mlalazi and Pathisa Nyathi.

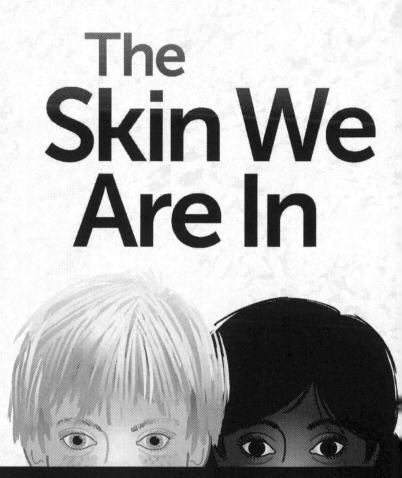

The Skin We Are In

Introducing a new book about the evolution of human skin colour!

Join Njabulo, Aisha, Tim, Chris and Roshni as they discover why humans have different skins, and how people's thinking about skin colour has changed throughout history. *The Skin We Are In* is a celebration of the glorious human rainbow, both in South Africa and beyond.

by Sindiwe Magona and Nina G. Jablonski

Illustrated by Lynn Fellman

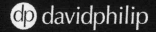

dp davidphilip

Amalion Publishing

Physical address	133 Cité Assembleé Ouakam BP 5637
	Dakar-Fann
	Dakar
Website	www.amalion.net
Email	publish@amalion.net
Phone	+221 33 860 1904
Facebook	AmalionPublishing
Twitter	Amalion
Contacts	Sulaiman Adebowale

Amalion Publishing is an independent scholarly publisher with the mission to disseminate innovative knowledge on Africa and to strengthen the understanding of Africa and its people. Amalion provides a platform for authors to express new, alternative and daring perspectives and views on people, places, events, and issues shaping our world. Amalion Publishing produces monographs, textbooks, journals and literary writing – primarily in English and French – for scholars, students, and general readers with an interest in African Studies, the Humanities, and the Social Sciences. Amalion titles are distributed in France and Benelux countries by l'Oiseau Indigo and Bookwitty (www.loiseauindigo.fr), in North America by International Specialized Book Services (www.isbs.com) and in the United Kingdom by Central Books (www.centralbooks.com).

Awesome SA

Physical address	29 Danville Ave
	Durban North
Postal Address	PO Box 121
	Glenashley
	4022
Website	www.awesomeSApublishers.com
Email	info@awesomesa.co.za
Phone	+27 82 786 8450
Contacts	Derryn Campbell

Awesome SA Publishers are independent publishers who create positive, non-fiction books which are interesting and engaging. First published in 2010 and again in 2015, the best-selling volumes of *Awesome South Africa* make the perfect gift for all

Awesome SA Publishers

ages. The colourful graphic design and photography within the books depict the heart and the soul of the country and are filled with fun, facts and humour and guaranteed to astonish and astound both South Africans and foreigners. The books created by Awesome SA Publishers invite the reader to positively influence the future. Visit our website to view the full range of books.

Ayebia

Physical address	7 Syringa Walk
	Banbury
	Oxfordshire
	OX16 1FR
Website	www.ayebia.co.uk
Email	ayebia@ayebia.co.uk
Phone	+44 1295 709228
Contacts	Nana Ayebia Clarke MBE
	(Managing Director)

Ayebia Clarke Publishing Limited is an award-winning independent publisher specializing in quality African and Caribbean literature based in Oxfordshire, UK. Ghanaian-born Publisher Becky Nana Ayebia Clarke was Submissions Editor at the highly regarded African and Caribbean Writers Series at Heinemann

Educational Books at Oxford for 12 years where she was part of a team in the International Department that published and promoted prominent and award-winning writers including Wole Soyinka, Ama Ata Aidoo, Chinua Achebe, Ngugi wa Thiong'o, Nadine Gordimer, *et al.* She founded Ayebia with her British husband David in 2003 as a way of looking to new directions in African publishing after Heinemann announced the demise of active publishing in the AWS in 2002. Ayebia's mission is to publish books that will open new spaces and bring fresh insights into African and Caribbean culture and literature internationally. Ayebia's books are currently used for courses on African Studies on Literature, History, Culture, Gender and Postcolonial courses internationally. Becky Nana Ayebia Clarke was awarded an Honorary MBE in 2011 by Her Majesty Queen Elizabeth II for 'services to the UK publishing industry.'

Basler Afrika Bibliographien

Physical address	Basler Afrika Bibliographien, Namibia Resource Centre – Southern Africa Library
	Publishing House BAB
	Klosterberg 21
Postal Address	PO Box 2037
	CH-4001 Basel
	Switzerland
Website	baslerafrika.ch
Email	publishing@baslerafrika.ch
Phone	+41 61 228 93 33

The BAB Publishing House has been publishing scholarly works on Southern Africa, especially Namibia, since 1971. Its thematic emphases are oriented towards the humanities and social sciences. The BAB Publishing House seeks to promote cultural exchange and engagement regarding important contemporary historical issues and, in particular, to provide African scholars with a platform. Our (cultural-) historical, political and anthropological publications are aimed at international academic audiences as well as engaged readers broadly interested in Africa.

Big Bug Books

Physical	6 Schroder Street
address	Stellenbosch
Website	www.bb-books.co.za
Email	paula@bb-books.co.za
Phone	+27 82 882 3923
Twitter	BigBugBookscc
Contacts	Paula Raubenheimer

Big Bug Books is a graded educational reading and life-skills series for children, ages 5–12 years, featuring the characters KIERIE & KRIEKIE®. The following languages are supported: Afrikaans, Chichewa, English, Hausa, Igbo, isiXhosa, isiZulu, Kinyarwanda, Kiswahili, Luganda, Luo, Shona and Yoruba. Paula Raubenheimer, an occupational therapist wrote and illustrated the readers and Dr. Hannie Menkveld, a foundation/elementary phase educator wrote the teacher manuals. The readers and teacher manuals have free worksheets. All material is available on tablet and mobile phone. We are committed to eradicating illiteracy.

BK Publishing

Physical address	1239 Francis Baard Street
	Hatfield
	Pretoria
	0083
Postal Address	P.O. Box 6314
	Pretoria
	0001
Websites	www.bkpublishing.co.za, www.supernovamagazine.co.za, www.preflightbooks.co.za
Email	mail@bkpublishing.com
Phone	+27 12 342 5347
Contacts	Benoit Knox
	(Director/Publisher)

BK Publishing is a vibrant publishing house in the heart of Pretoria. Our entrepreneurial spirit has manifested itself in the great variety of projects, imprints and services we provide. To fulfil our vision of fostering a book loving and book buying culture, we have created *Supernova*, the magazine for curious kids. With *Supernova* and other products for reluctant readers, we aim to make children aware of issues which affect them, their community and their environment. We give them the tools and inspiration to become active and responsible world citizens. With over 10 years of experience and a collection of wonderful original publications, our indie imprint, Preflight Books, helps aspiring authors and self-publishers bring their manuscripts to life.

Black Letter Media

Physical address	1st Flr Metropolitan Park
	Regus Business Centre
	8 Hillside Road
	Parktown
Postal Address	P.O. Box 94004
	Yeoville
	2198
Website	www.blackletterm.com
Email	info@blackletterm.com
Phones	+27 84 849 8670, +011 480 4993
Facebook	BlackLetterMedia
Twitter	blklettermedia
Contacts	Duduzile Mabaso

Black Letter Media is a publishing and story development company which focuses on creating platforms online or in print for new African storytellers to publish their vision of Africa and for African readers to discover, new, independent

African literature. We do this through platforms such as poetrypotion.com, and print books including the Poetry Potion quarterly, short story collections and novels, as well as developing stories for television. Our writers and publishers are primarily based in South African but include Nigeria, Uganda, Cameroon, Kenya, Zimbabwe, Uganda and Botswana.

ALBERTINA SISULU

ABRIDGED BY SINDIWE MAGONA
AND ELINOR SISULU

The latest biography of
Albertina Sisulu, mother of the nation.

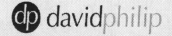

Book Dash

Website	www.bookdash.org
Email	team@bookdash.org
Facebook	bookdash
Twitter	bookdash
Instagram	bookdash
Contacts	Julia Norrish

At Book Dash, we believe every child should own a hundred books by the age of five. This means creating and distributing large numbers of new, African storybooks in local languages. To make this possible, we gather creative professionals to create high-quality children's books that anyone can freely download, print, translate and distribute. We then work with funders and literacy and ECD organisations to print and give away books in large volumes. Funders and partner organisations are encouraged to visit our website and get in contact with us.

Bookcraft

Physical address	23 Adebajo Street Kongi Layout Ibadan
Postal Address	GPO Box 16729 Dugbe Ibadan Oyo State
Website	www.bookcraftafrica.com
Email	info@bookcraftafrica.com
Phones	+234 8033447889, +234 8073199967, +234 8037220773
Facebook	BookcraftAfrica
Twitter	bookcraftafrica
Contacts	Dapo Olugbade

Bookcraft Ltd is a publishing company. We have published a large number of titles in a wide variety of subjects: art, biography, history, literature, politics, and current affairs. We publish for a growing market of discerning, sophisticated and well educated bibliophiles. Our books' uniquely packaged, reader friendly design makes them instantly recognizable.

Bookstorm

Physical address	2nd Floor, Blackheath Mews
	258 Beyers Naude Drive
	Blackheath
	2195
Postal Address	PO Box 4532
	Northcliff
	Johannesburg
	2115
Website	www.bookstorm.co.za
Email	info@bookstorm.co.za
Phone	+27 11 478 6020
Facebook	Bookstorm

Bookstorm is a boutique non-fiction book publishing company offering focused experience and innovation in the creation of books for the South African market. Bookstorm was founded in 2010 by Louise Grantham and Basil van Rooyen, both experienced trade publishers with a long history of publishing for the South African general reading market. We publish in a variety of genres including business, entrepreneurship, economics, investment, current affairs, cookery, health, sports and travel. Our books are written by a range of select South African authors who represent a diversity of skills and opinions. Bookstorm also offers agency distribution, corporate publishing services, and self-publishing services under its Rainbird imprint.

Breeze Publishing

Physical address	15 Lavery Crescent
	Overport
	4091
	Durban
Email	breezepublishing@gmail.com
Phone	+27 791079930
Facebook	breezepublishingcc
Contacts	Naseema Mall

Breeze Publishing is set on publishing quality books of a variety of themes and categories, both in fiction and non-fiction; for the adult, teen and children's markets. Breeze Publishing is constantly  being approached by both local and foreign authors, and continues to carefully select manuscripts of quality. The company has great aspirations to become a dominant player in a very versatile but restricted market and hopes to affiliate itself with both budding as well as established authors, so that it can grow with them to greater heights.

Burnet Media

Postal Address	PO Box 53557
	Kenilworth
	7745
	Cape Town
Website	www.burnetmedia.co.za
Email	info@burnetmedia.co.za
Facebook	TwoDogsMercury
Twitter	BurnetMedia
Contacts	Tim Richman

Burnet Media is an independent publisher based in Cape Town. We produce books for two main imprints – Two Dogs and Mercury, established in 2006 and 2011 respectively – as well as various customised publishing projects. As an authors' publisher our aim is to build close and interactive relationships with our authors and clients and, in doing so, create interesting and innovative titles for South Africa and the world. Jacana Media markets our titles into the trade.

Cassava Republic

Physical address	62B Arts and Crafts Village Opposite Sheraton Hotel Abuja
Website	www.cassavarepublic.biz
Email	editor@cassavarepublic.biz
Phone	+234 09 780 3159
Facebook	CassavaRepublic
Twitter	CassavaRepublic
Contacts	Bibi Bakare-Yusuf

We publish literary fiction, non-fiction, crime fiction, children's and young adult fiction and non-fiction. We also have a romance series published under the imprint Ankara Press.

cassavarepublic
seeding the African imagination

all about writing

courses for people passionate about writing

Take your writing to the next level

Creative Writing Course

Learn all the skills you need to write fiction or creative non-fiction

- 10 modules
- 2 to 3 hours a week
- Full personal feedback

Mentoring, coaching and literary reports

- Structural, narrative, plot and characterisation assessment
- Practical advice on where a manuscript works, where it doesn't, and how to mend its flaws.

Catalyst Press

UNITED STATES

Postal Address	2941 Kelly Street
	Livermore
	CA 94551
Website	www.catalystpress.org
Email	info@catalystpress.org
Phone	+1 925 315 5970
Facebook	catalystbooks2
Twitter	catalyst_press
Instagram	catalystpress
Contacts	Jessica Powers

Catalyst Press is an independent publishing company founded in 2017. At Catalyst, we see books as a spark for change in the world. We seek to publish books that reveal the world from different perspectives, tilting or reversing or tweaking our own understanding of what's real,

CATALYST PRESS

true, necessary, or beautiful.Catalyst's publishing program emphasizes books emerging from the African continent and about Africa but not exclusively; we plan to expand to publishing indigenous writers from other parts of the world, all with the goal of publishing literature that exposes the truth and pursues justice and peace. North-American based Catalyst Press is distributed throughout Southern Africa by Lapa Uitgewers - lapa@lapa.co.za

Chimurenga

Physical address	Room 303
	Pan African Market
	76 Long Street
	Cape Town
Postal Address	PO Box 15117
	Vlaeberg
	8018
	Cape Town
Website	www.chimurenga.co.za
Emails	chimurenga@panafrican.co.za, info@chimurenga.co.za
Phone	+27 21 422 4168
Facebook	Chimurenga
Twitter	Chimurenga_SA

Chimurenga is a journal of writing, art, culture and politics published out of Cape Town. Since its first issue (2002), *Chimurenga* has received excellent reviews for its originality, the quality of its content and its willingness to tackle subjects other publications might consider too difficult or controversial to address. Moreover, several contributors have won international awards for their work published in *Chimurenga*: Binyavanga Wainaina, Yvonne Adhiambo Owuor, Ishtiyaq Shukri, Chimamanda Ngozi Adichie and Seffi Atta to name a few.

Clockwork Books

SOUTH AFRICA

Postal Address	PO Box 44224
	Linden
	2104
Website	www.ClockworkBooks.co.za
Email	info@worktheclock.co.za
Phone	+27 10 900 3164
Facebook	ClockworkBooksZA
Contacts	Sarah McGregor

Passionate about the exceptional fiction and nonfiction emerging from South Africa, Clockwork Books is an independent publisher, online book store, and publishing services provider.

A virtual hub servicing authors and readers alike, we aim to revolutionise the local publishing landscape while empowering our authors to be in control of their work and enhancing the connection between creators and their communities.

Cover2Cover

Physical address	85 Main Road
	Muizenberg
	Cape Town
	7945
Website	cover2cover.co.za
Email	info@cover2cover.co.za
Phone	+27 21 709 0128
Facebook	cover2cover1
Twitter	Cover2CoverB

Cover2Cover Books aims to get young South Africans reading by publishing exciting stories that relate to their lives. Our flagship series, Harmony High, is set in a fictional township high school, and follows the lives, loves and challenges of a group of young people. Cover2Cover continues to grow, and is currently launching two new series – Soccer Season, set in a teen soccer club, and Shadow Chasers, a fantasy series aimed at readers of 8–12 year olds. We also publish FunDza's exciting short story anthologies as well as YA trade fiction. Our non-fiction imprint, Face2Face, showcases South African memoirs, continuing in our tradition of publishing uniquely South African stories.

Cover2Cover has also published isiXhosa and isiZulu anthologies of short stories for teens and young adults. Shadow Chasers, our 'tween' series, is available in isiZulu, and our new series, Jabulani Junior, uses cartoon, English and isiXhosa to tell its stories aimed at ages 8-10 years.

David Philip Publishers

Physical address	2nd Floor
	6 Spin Street
	Cape Town
	8001
Website	www.newafricabooks.co.za
Email	info@newafricabooks.co.za
Phone	+27 21 467 5860
Facebook	DavidPhilipPublishers
Twitter	_DavidPhilipPub
Instagram	newafricabooks
Contacts	Dusanka Stojakovic

New Africa Books, incorporating David Philip Publishers, is one of South Africa's oldest and most prestigious independent publishing houses. With a history stretching back over 45 years, New Africa Books currently publishes literary and educational books for adults, children and young adults in all South African languages. Focusing on younger readers, our latest releases include the non-fiction children's book, *Skin we are in,* about the science behind skin colour; the illustrated children's book *Mpumi's Magic Beads* written by Lebohang Masango and the latest biography of Mam Sisulu called *Mam Sisulu, Albertina Sisulu: Abridged Memoir,* written by Sindiwe Magona and Elinor Sisulu. We are also proud to publish the celebrated African superhero comic series, *Kwezi.* We have a treasure trove of great books for adults, written by a number of well-known authors, including Richard Rive and Nick Mulgrew.

Mpumi's magic beads

AVAILABLE IN ALL ELEVEN OFFICIAL SOUTH AFRICAN LANGUAGES

ENGLISH

ISIZULU

XITSONGA

ISIXHOSA

Written by

Lebohang Masango

with illustrations by Masego Morulane

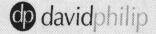
davidphilip

info@newafricabooks.co.za | www.newafricabooks.com

Deep South

Postal Address   PO Box 6082 Market Square Grahamstown 6141
Email   r.berold@gmail.com
Phone   +27 46 622 5081
Contacts   Robert Berold

Deep South specialises in South African writing, mostly poetry. The press is run by Robert Berold. Local distribution is handled by University of KwaZulu-Natal Press and international distribution is handled by African Books Collective. 21 titles have been published since 2000 including books by Seitlhamo Motsapi, Ari Sitas, Angifi Dladla, Joan Metelerkamp, Kelwyn Sole, Kobus Moolman, Khulile Nxumalo, Mzwandile Matiwana, Mishka Hoosen, Mxolisi Nyewa, Vonani Bila and Lesego Rampolokeng.

Dryad Press

Postal Address	Postnet Suite 281
	Private Bag X16
	Constantia, Cape Town
	7848
Website	dryadpress.co.za
Email	business@dryadpress.co.za
Facebook	DryadPress
Twitter	DryadPress
Instagram	DryadPresssa
Contacts	Michèle Betty

Dryad Press is an independent press dedicated to the promotion and publication of poetry in South Africa. It is a literary collaboration between Michèle Betty (editor of New Contrast: South African Literary Journal) and Joan Hambidge (renowned poet, literary critic, academic and Professor at the University of Cape Town). Dryad Press seeks to publish poetry, which in the words of Barthes, searches for "the inalienable meaning of things". Innovative and exciting poetry with the power to defamiliarise, to surprise, not only in form and technique, but also in its capacity to enable us to reflect on our experiences in the world in a new way.

Éditions Graines de Pensées

Physical	30
address	Boulevard du 13 Janvier
	Nyékonakpoè – Lomé 07 B.P. 7097
Website	www.afrilivres.net
Email	grainesdepensees@yahoo.com
Phones	+228 90 32 33 20, +228 22 22 32 43
Facebook	editions.grainesdepensees
Twitter	gpensees
Contacts	Mrs Yasmin Issaka-Coubageat

At Graines de Pensées we want to participate in African cultural expression, to contribute, with our books, to the development of a democratic and pluralist society, with the ability to criticize and respond to social issues. As publishers we are keen to give to this new African generation books that are accessible, that they can relate to, and that have a very high editorial quality. Furthermore, for a better distribution of our books, we participate in co-publishing projects, with partners in countries in both the South and the North. We also create business relationships with various institutions and companies for the better promotion of books in French, English and African languages.

Femrite – Uganda Women Writers Association

Physical address	Kira Road Plot 147 705 Kampala
Website	www.femriteug.org
Email	info@femriteug.org
Phone	+256 414 543 943
Facebook	FemriteUg
Twitter	ugwomenwriters
Contacts	Hilda Twongyeirwe (Executive Director)

FEMRITE publishes fiction and creative non-fiction which is mainly written by women. From establishment, the organization was aimed at training, promoting and publishing women writers. This still has a big bearing on what is published because women's situations which led to the establishing of the organization have not changed substantially. However, FEMRITE has included male writers in its programmes because both male and female writers operate under the same infrastructure and some issues such as limited publishing opportunities affect them in the same way.

Fundza Literacy Trust

Physical address	85 Main Road
	Muizenberg
	Cape Town
Website	http://www.fundza.co.za/
Email	info@fundza.co.za
Phone	+27 21 709 0688
Facebook	FunDzaLiteracyTrust
Twitter	FunDzaClub
Contact	Mignon Hardie, Zilungile Zimela

The FunDza Literacy Trust believes that reading changes lives. Its mission is to get young South Africans - specifically those from poor backgrounds with little access to books - reading and writing for pleasure. Through FunDza's 'cellphone library' - fundza.mobi - it is creating, commissioning, curating and publishing new local stories, books, blogs and articles to inspire a lifelong love of reading and stories. More than 200,000 unique users connect with FunDza's network every month.

FunDza's innovative approach to developing readers and writers has received local and international recognition. In 2017, it was awarded the inaugural Joy of Reading Award, a Gold Impumelelo Social Innovation Award, and the UNESCO Confucius Prize for Literacy.

Geko Publishing

Physical address	40 Morsim Road
	Hyde Park
	Johannesburg
Website	gekopublishing.co.za
Email	write@gekopublishing.co.za
Phone	+27 83 991 6647
Facebook	GekoPublishingSA
Twitter	GekoPublishing
Contacts	Phehello Mofokeng

We publish what makes us happy – from poetry, music biographies, fiction (novels, short stories etc.), fantasy and most importantly folklore/folktales in English and in African languages. Go to our website to download or read submission guidelines before submitting anything.

geko publishing
freedom to write.

Groenheide Boeke

Postal Address	PO Box 508
	Hartenbos 6520
	South Africa
Website	www.groenheide.co.za
Email	admin@groenheide.co.za
Facebook	groenheideboeke

Groenheide Boeke se ideaal is om met die medewerking van beide gevestigde en nuwe skrywers bekostigbare boeke aan te bied wat in elke opsig van net so 'n hoogstaande gehalte as enige duur boek is wat deur die groot uitgewers gepubliseer word. Ons reken dat Afrikaanse lektuur vandag vir baie persone, veral kinders en afgetredenes, te duur geword het en ons glo dat teen minder as R100 – dikwels selfs minder as R50 – vir 'n gedrukte boek ons die genot van lees weer binne die bereik van almal stel.

Groenheide Boeke publiseer enkelboeke en reekse. Ons publiseer nuwe boeke, asook boeke wat uit kopiereg en nie meer beskikbaar is nie. Ons gewildste reekse is die verskeie *Heideroos Romanses* (liefdesverhale vir alle ouderdomme), *Die Poniehoewe-Klub* (vir meisies 9 tot 12 jaar wat mal is oor perde), *Die Karoo Avonture* (plaaslike 'cowboy'-boeke vir seuns en mans) en klassieke Afrikaanse reekse soos *Die Swart Luiperd* en *Temmers van die Woestyn*.

Besoek Groenheide Boeke se webwerf vir al die inligting rakende publikasie van manuskripte of die aankoop van boeke, hetsy vir eie leesgenot of herverkoop in winkels.

Happy Readers

Physical address	23 Guys Cliff
	Harare
	Zimbabwe
Postal Address	P.O. Box BW 773
	Borrowdale
	Harare
	Zimbabwe
Website	www.happy-readers.com
Emails	happybooks.emma@gmail.com,
	happybooks.conor@gmail.com
Phones	+263 77 238 6163, +263 04 88 37 35
Facebook	happyreaderszimbabwe
Twitter	HappyReadersZim
Contacts	Emma O'Beirne

Happy Readers are all you need to read! A specifically structured reading program for children with ESOL – books, teacher training, class resources and M & E implementation in conjunction with donor partners. Primarily aimed at Grades 1 and 2, but frequently used throughout schools as remedial readers. Our books are fun, happy, brightly coloured and use animals as characters in familiar rural and urban settings. Happy Readers promote positive African values as well as sensitising children and teachers to gender-specific issues, best cultural practices and better-world themes. Ministry of Education approved for use in schools in Zimbabwe and Zambia.

Helco Promotions

Physical address	61 Quarrywood
	13 The Straight
	Lonehill
	2191
Email	info@helco.co.za
Phone	+27 82 452 9488
Facebook	HelcoPromotions
Twitter	HelcoPromotions
Instagram	holyoakeh
Contacts	Helen Holyoake

Helco Promotions is a full-range public-relations and communications company. We deal with clients from across the board for PR and communications campaigns that are focused, objective and results oriented. In addition to conventional PR clients, we are always looking to take on books, authors and events for PR and marketing. Here we bring to bear our wealth of experience with a tight and well-managed network of media contacts. Be it fiction or non-fiction, a conference on archeology or a foreign-language author, we have the experience to leverage their news into the South African media market in a way that is efficient, clear and far-reaching.

Huza Press

Physical address	Street KN 14
	House No. 21
	Kigali
Postal Address	PO Box 1610
	Kigali
Website	www.huzapress.com
Email	huzapress@gmail.com
Phone	+25 7810181278
Facebook	Huzapress
Twitter	huzapress
Instagram	huzapress
Contacts	Louise Umutoni-Bower

Huza Press is a literary publisher based in Kigali committed to the production and dissemination of knowledge through literature in Africa. We published our first title in 2017 (*Versus and Other Stories*). Over the next five years we are committed to building a commercially sustainable list of the best contemporary Rwandan and African writing, and working innovatively to make this widely available in Rwanda, East Africa and beyond.

impepho press

Postal Address	PO Box 12258
	Queenswood
	Pretoria
	0121
Website	www.impephopress.co.za
Email	getinfo@impephopress.co.za
Phone	+27 82 330 7249
Facebook	impephop
Twitter	impephop

impepho press is a Pan Africanist publishing house committed to the sincere telling of African and international stories, celebrating both the fragility and resilience of the human experience. We believe in championing brave, particularly feminist, voices committed to literary excellence.

We pride ourselves on providing our authors with the best editorial, design and promotional support as possible, irrespective of the stages in their careers. At impepho press, we serve the stories, always! Because without our stories, we would, in the words of Audre Lorde, be crumpled into other people's fantasies of us and eaten alive.

Junkets Publisher

Postal Address	PO Box 38040
	Pinelands
	Cape Town
	7430
Website	www.junkets.co.za
Email	info.junkets@iafrica.com
Phones	+27 78 763 3177, +27 76 169 2789
Facebook	groups/Junkets, Junketspublisher, Junkets10Series
Contact	Andi Mgibantaka, Robin Malan

Junkets Publisher is a small not-for-profit independent publisher that specialises in high-quality low-cost new South African playscripts. We publish the Playscript Series of individual plays, the Collected Series of anthologies of plays, and the Junkets10Series of ten new plays celebrating our tenth birthday in 2015. The BaxterJunkets series publishes the winning play of each year's Zabalaza Theatre Festival. GayJunkets publishes queer-interest books in various genres. The first book we published in 2005 was *Rebel Angel,* a novel based on the life of John Keats. 'Junkets' is Leigh Hunt's nickname for him: Jun-Kets. Our logo is Keats's autograph.

Junkets Publisher

Kachifo

Physical address	253 Herbert Macaulay Way
	Yaba
	Lagos
Websites	www.kachifo.com, farafinabooks.wordpress.com
Email	info@kachifo.com
Phone	+23 48077364217
Facebook	farafinabook
Twitter	farafinabooks

Kachifo Limited, an independent Nigerian publishing house, began operations in 2004 driven by the words of its motto and mission statement, Telling our own Stories. Its imprint, Farafina, has published works of fiction, memoirs, and poetry with an African audience in mind. It continues to receive unsolicited submissions at submissions@kachifo.com.

Kalahari Publishers and Booksellers

SOUTH AFRICA

Physical address	116 ERF Mphaphuli Makwarela Road Next to Exel Sibasa 0970
Website	www.kpb.co.za
Email	info@kpb.co.za
Phone	+27 15 963 1529
Contacts	Themba Patrick Magaisa (Xitsonga Publisher)

Khaloza Books

Physical address	6 Frolich Street
	Parys
	Free State
Postal Address	PO Box 998
	Parys
	Free State
	9585
Website	www.khalozabooks.com
Email	info@khalozabooks.com
Contacts	Thato Motaung
	(Managing Editor)

Khaloza Books is a publishing company established in 2017, as a Pan-African publishing house for books – fiction and non-fiction – about Africa for children and young adults. We believe in producing and celebrating African literature, whilst preserving values of Pan-Africanism, a respect for people and nature, and a commitment to pushing boundaries. We aim to encourage everyone to Read.Write.African

Kwani Trust

Postal Address	PO Box 2895-00100
	Nairobi
	Kenya
Website	www.kwani.org
Email	sales@kwani.org
Phones	+254 70 483 2379, +254 20 444 1801
Facebook	kwanitrust
Twitter	kwanitrust

Kwani Trust is a regional literary hub and a community of writers that is committed to the growth of the region's creative industry through publishing and distributing contemporary African literature, offering training opportunities, producing literary events and establishing global literary networks.

Kwarts Publishers

Physical address	37 Beverly Hills Crescent Centurion Golf Estate 0157
Website	www.kwartspublishers.co.za
Email	info@kwartspublishers.co.za
Phone	+27 12 752 5877
Facebook	kwartspublishers
Contacts	Anita Stander

Kwarts Publishers offers a range of professional services to assist independent authors in getting their books published in digital as well as printed format. Our services include cover design, page layout and type-setting, e-book production, ISBN registration and printing. We publish books in various genres and are committed to providing authors with quality products that have great marketing potential. We pride ourselves in offering excellent book design services and cost effective printing solutions. Member of PASA since 2011.

Kwarts 🜨
PUBLISHERS

Kwasukela Books

Physical address	4 Boundary Road, Newlands, Cape Town
	Newlands
	Cape Town
Postal Address	9 Flamboyant Avenue
	Westbrook
	Othongathi
	4400
Website	www.kwasukelabook.com
Email	wade@kwasukelabooks.com
Phone	+27 81 039 5902
Facebook	kwasukelabooks
Twitter	kwasukelabooks
Instagram	kwasukelabooks
Contacts	Wade Smit

Kwasukela Books publishes mainly isiZulu fiction, particularly that which is in some way innovative or changes the landscape of South African literature. Our first book, a collection of short stories entitled Izinkanyezi Ezintsha, showcased seven pieces of speculative fiction, making it the first speculative-fiction collection of short stories in isiZulu. We believe that the literary world in South Africa is still feeling the effects of our history of oppression, and publishing new voices in South African languages is an integral part of feeling represented in the content we produce as a country.

Les Classiques Africains

Physical address	25 Club Road
	Vacoas
	Mauritius
Website	www.lesclassiquesafricains.com
Email	info@lesclassiquesafricains.com
Phone	+230 601 14 84
Facebook	les.classiques.africains

Originally a French publishing house, Les Classiques Africains was bought in 2006 by a Mauritian company. Renowned all over Frenchspeaking African countries for more than 50 years, our catalogue now offers more than 200 titles in various fields: school textbooks, practical guides, religious books and children's books. Based in Mauritius, our team is dedicated to publishing affordable books of excellent quality.

Life Righting Collective

Physical address	121 Runciman Drive
	Simon's Town
	Cape Town
	7975
Website	www.liferighting.com
Email	info@liferighting.com
Phone	+27 83 446 1161
Contacts	Dawn Garisch

The Life Righting Collective runs courses for anyone who wants to learn to write about their experiences. Our approach promotes self-discovery, self-recovery and more effective communication. We raise funds to make courses available to those in need of sponsorship and to provide platforms for these life stories to be published. Our website and our first publication, *This is how it is*, published in partnership with Jacana's Fanele imprint, are our main calling cards. Sharing experiences with a wide readership can help reduce discrimination and promote mutual understanding.

Liquid Type Publishing Services

Physical address	1891 Hearn Road
	Henley on Klip
	Midvaal
	1961
Postal Address	P.O. Box 448
	Henley on Klip
	1962
Website	www.liquidtype.co.za
Email	wesley@liquidtype.co.za
Phone	+27 72 649 5274
Twitter	liquidType
Contacts	Wesley Thompson

Liquid Type Publishing Services is a specialised book-publishing services company that offers exceptional editing, ebook design, project management, proofreading and self-publishing services to authors, companies and publishers. Liquid Type's work is characterised by fine attention to detail, sound publishing advice and the highest book-production standards. Please contact me to discuss all things bookish.

MaThoko's Books

Postal Address	PO Box 31719
	Braamfontein
	2017
Website	www.gala.co.za
Email	info@gala.co.za
Phone	+27 11 717 4239
Facebook	MathokosBooks

MaThoko's Books is the publishing imprint of Gay and Lesbian Memory in Action (GALA). Launched in 2011, the imprint aims to be a corrective to the limited publishing support for queer writing in Africa and to act as a springboard for emerging and marginalised voices. It also provides a much-needed publishing outlet for scholarly works on LGBTIQ-related themes. MaThoko's Books was founded on a belief that the sharing of stories can help to challenge homophobia and transphobia. The imprint is committed to publishing high-quality writing that not only helps to educate the public about sexuality and gender identity but that also promotes human rights on the African continent.

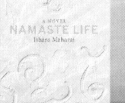

MBLS Publishing

SOUTH AFRICA

Physical address	45 Balsam Street
	Zakariyya Park
	1829
Postal Address	P O Box 21758
	Zakariyya Park
	1821
Website	www.mbls.co.za
Email	mbls.publishing@gmail.com
Phone	+27 11 859 2471
Facebook	MBLS-Publishing-318042515064830

MBLS Publishing publishes children's book under the imprints THEMBI AND THEMBA BOOKS, AYANDA BOOKS and LEARN TO READ – READ TO LEARN for reading at the library and to educate in the classroom; informing and educating children about institutions and societal issues to contribute to their development as caring and responsible young adults.

Modjaji Books

Postal Address	PO Box 121
	Rondebosch
	7701
	Cape Town
Website	www.modjajibooks.co.za
Email	info@modjajibooks.co.za
Phone	+ 27 72 774 3546
Facebook	Modjajibooks
Twitter	modjaji_bks
Contacts	Colleen Higgs

An independent publishing company based in Cape Town, South Africa. We publish books by southern African women writers. We publish novels, short stories, memoir, biography, poetry, essays, narrative non-fiction and award-winning women writers with brave voices. The history of publishing in South Africa is enmeshed with the culture of resistance that flourished under apartheid. 'Struggle' literature may have emerged from the 'underground', but women's voices – particularly black women's voices – are still marginalised. Modjaji Books addresses this inequality by publishing books that are true to the spirit of Modjaji the rain queen: a powerful female force for good, growth, new life, regeneration. Our books are distributed locally by Protea Boekehuis into the trade. LAPA Uitgewers distribute to schools in South Africa. African Books Collective distribute our titles internationally.

Poetree Publications

Physical address	217 Textile House
	125 Kerk Street
	Johannesburg
	2000
Email	poetflow@live.com
Phone	+27 73 652 0275
Facebook	poetreepub
Twitter	PoetreeBooks
Contacts	Selome Payne (Flow)

Poetree Publications strives to provide affordable and accessible publishing services to writers of all genres, and change the perceptions of self-publishing as a whole. The mission is to make a significant contribution to the amount of new and modern written works within the literature industry, primarily in the African literature scene. Poetree aims to immortalise and preserve the stories and indigenous languages of writers, especially the youth, by offering self-publishing services for poetry, fiction/non-fiction, children's stories, motivational books, short stories and more. Services include publishing in print and e-formats.

Poets Printery

Physical address	1 Saint David Road
	Selborne
	5201
	East London
Postal Address	PO Box 1250
	Amalinda
	5252
	East London
Websites	www.poetsprintery.co.za, www.amitabhmitra.com, poetsprintery.bookslive.co.za
Email	amitabh@amitabhmitra.com
Phone	+27 82 202 6155
Facebook	groups/123212177694162
Twitter	amitabhmitra
Contacts	Dr Amitabh Mitra

We are publishing up and coming Southern African and South Asian poets. We are into poetry-art and poetry cinema too. We publish coffee table books of visual arts. Our books are available locally and on Amazon.

Porcupine Press

Physical address	No. 2 Anikehof Complex, Martha Road North (off Rabie Road)
	Fontainebleau
	Randburg
	2194
Postal Address	PO Box 2756
	Pinegowrie
	2123
Website	www.porcupinepress.co.za
Phone	+27 11 791 4561
Facebook	PorcupinePressPage
Twitter	Porcupine_PRESS
Contacts	Gail Robbins

Independent publishing since 2009. Ask your self-publishers how they make their money. What percentage comes from book production? What percentage comes from book sales? Now ask Porcupine the same question. The answer is: throughout 2015 the split was 50/50. We sell what we produce because: • Quality is our non-negotiable. Quality content – quality design – quality printing • Our distribution works. We deal directly with all major bookshop chains and independents – we offer international services – we know how to work the e-book markets. We also distribute for other small publishers and independent authors.

SA Book Development Council

Physical address	Tijger Park 3, 2nd Floor, Room 202
	Willie van Schoor
	Bellville
	7530
Postal Address	PO Box 583
	Sanlamhof
	7532
Website	www.sabookcouncil.co.za
Email	admin@sabookcouncil.co.za
Phone	+27 21 914 8626
Contacts	Raynia Gaffoor

The Indigenous Languages Publishing Programme is one of the SABDC's programmes to stimulate growth and development in the sector. It aims to increase indigenous languages publishing and to support the ongoing production of South-African-authored books in the local languages. The SABDC bi-annually invites registered publishing companies to submit applications for the publishing of children and youth creative works (including novels, short stories, children's literature, etc.) Each submission should be an original work written in one of 9 local languages. (Excluding Afrikaans and English), This programme also contributes to the transformation imperatives of the SABDC. More information on the programme is available on the website.

SOUTH AFRICAN
BOOK DEVELOPMENT
COUNCIL

SAfAIDS Materials Development and Production Services

Physical address	17 Beveridge Road
	Avondale
	Harare
Website	www.safaids.net
Email	katrina@safaids.net
Phone	+263 4 336193
Twitter	SAfAIDS
Contacts	Katrina Wallace-Karenga

We promote: effective and ethical development responses on SRHR, HIV and TB prevention, treatment and care. We provide: complete information and communications packages, as well as in-house services such as: training and facilitation; editing, content development, translation, design and layout; professional management of the print finish on all products; excellence in targeted information development and production, enabling you to communicate effectively with your target audience through services from:

- Branding;
- Conceptualisation and content development;
- Editing;
- Translation and back translation;
- Design and layout; to
- Final production and printing.

SEDIA

Physical address	Cité les mandariniers, Lot 293
	Al Mohammadia
	16211
	Alger
Postal Address	BP 231
	Al Mohammadia
Website	www.sedia-dz.com
Email	sedia@sedia-dz.com
Phone	+213 770 973 861
Facebook	sediaalgiers
Contacts	Nacéra Khiat

SEDIA is an Algerian publishing house created in March, 2000 known for editing curricular and extra-curricular books before becoming in 2006 a non-specialized publishing house with the peculiarity to republish famous Algerian novelists from abroad as their several translated work, such as Mohammed Dib and Assia Djebar. With its rich and varied catalog, between novels, essays, beautiful books and comic books besides preschool methods and extracurricular books, SEDIA detains a considerable place in the field of the Algerian books today not only as publisher but also as importer of books.

Société d'Edition et de Diffusion Internationale Algérienne

Sefsafa Culture & Publishing

Physical address	4 Soliman Gohar Sq. Dokki Giza
Website	www.sefsafa.net
Emails	elbaaly@gmail.com, info@sefsafa.net
Phones	+201110787870, +201275324306
Facebook	sefsafa
Twitter	Sefsafapub
Contacts	Mohamed El-Baaly

Sefsafa Culture & Publishing is a small group based in Egypt, working under the umbrella of 'Sefsafa Culture & Publishing'. We have had a publishing house since 2009, and have published over 100 titles, one third of them translations. The group has also organized the Cairo Literature Festival since 2015, and the Egypt Comix Week festival since 2014. Sefsafa aims to support the enlightenment and Arab Spring ideals.

Sera Blue

Physical address	46 Belvedere Road
	Glen Austin AH
	Midrand
Website	www.serablue.com
Email	hello@serablue.com
Facebook	serabluepublishing
Twitter	SeraBluePublish
Instagram	sera_blue_publishing
Contacts	Kelan Gerriety

Sera Blue is a vibrant publisher based in Midrand, South Africa. We are a small team of multi-skilled professionals who are passionate about books. We provide a personal and creative publishing experience for our authors and we believe in the final work staying true to the author's vision. We pour our focus into

genre fiction such as fantasy, horror and sci-fi, as well as the many subgenres from there. We believe every person has a story to tell and in 2016 we opened our doors to help authors bring their fiction stories to life.

Shama Books

Postal Address	PO Box 57
	Piazza
	in front of Cathedral School
	Addis Ababa
Website	www.shamaethiopia.com
Emails	shama@ethionet.et, gbagersh@shamaethipia.com
Phone	+251 11 554 5290
Contacts	Ghassan Bagersh

Shama Books, fully owned by the Bagersh family, has been involved in the publishing of books since 1999, making it the premier mass market publisher in Ethiopia. Shama boasts a burgeoning publishing house that attracts the finest Ethiopian writers, as well as many established foreign authors. Shama,

with a mission of improving literacy at all levels and fostering a reading culture in the country, has published over a hundred titles. In addition to operating a chain of BookWorld bookshops we also operate newsstands and souvenir shops in the major five star hotels in Addis Ababa.

Siber Ink

Postal Address	PO Box 30702
	Tokai
	7966
Website	www.siberink.co.za
Email	simon@siberink.co.za
Phone	+27 21 712 1500
Facebook	SiberInk
Twitter	SiberInk
Contacts	Simon Sephton

Siber Ink was founded in 2000 by Simon Sephton after 17 years in corporate law publishing as a niche firm focusing on publishing **relevant, accessible and authoritative law and business texts.** We publish relevant materials that are based on law for non-lawyers (eg labour law for the HR sector and Unions); law texts for students & practitioners; and regular updates in certain sectors of law. Our books strive to be easily read and highly authoritative.

Sooo Many Stories

Physical address	Plot 3003 Bbuye Ntinda
Postal Address	P.O. Box 3057
Website	somanystories.ug
Email	kaboozi@somanystories.ug
Phone	+25 670 571 1442
Facebook	sooomanystories
Contacts	Nyana Kakoma

Sooo Many Stories started as a blog with the sole aim of showcasing Ugandan Literature. 18 months later the blog morphed into a publishing house and published its first title in June 2016. They are passionate about making literature accessible to as many people as possible and helping reluctant readers realise that reading can be fun.

Sooo Many Stories also runs book clubs for children and adults (as a YouTube channel: #MEiREAD) and runs a children library as well.

South African Heritage Publishers

Physical address	14 Zen
	1 Harper Road
	Bedfordview
Postal Address	PO Box 3048
	Bedfordview
	2008
Website	www.saheritagepublishers.co.za
Email	info@saheritagepublishers.co.za
Twitter	saheritagepub

South Africans know little of their own past let alone that of other South Africans who have a different language as mother tongue. Conceived in rural Vuwani during a discussion between four friends - a Tshivenda speaker, two Xitsonga speakers, one of Vhatsonga heritage the other amaShangaan, and an English speaking South African - on the first meeting of their ancestors and the role of the Portuguese in those early encounters. Written in English to ensure accessibility Our Story is designed to be read in the language classroom to improve literacy while providing valuable information to young and older readers. Each story is restricted to 10 000 words and 48 beautifully illustrated pages. See our website for extracts from these titles.

South African National Lexicography Units

Physical address	14 Zen
	1 Harper Road
	Bedfordview
Postal Address	PO Box 3048
	Bedfordview
	2008
Website	www.lexiunitsa.org
Email	info@lexiunitsa.org

The nine indigenous language National Lexicography Units, supported by the Pan South African Language Board, have a Constitutional and Legislative mandate to develop dictionaries and other material in our indigenous languages which when used "will elevate their status and advance their use" while ensuring that "no language is disadvantaged over any other". The material we produce is designed to create a more multilingual and socially cohesive society while supporting IL speakers to learn English. Copyright in our dictionaries is held by the Units on behalf of the State. The dictionaries are a national language resource in our languages. We are currently developing material in the San, Nama and Khoi languages.

Story Press Africa

Postal Address	P.O. Box 22106
	Mayor's Walk
	3208
Website	www.storypressafrica.com
Email	info@storypressafrica.com
Phone	+27 76 173 7130
Facebook	storypressafrica
Twitter	catalyst_press
Instagram	catalystpress
Contacts	Robert Inglis

Story Press Africa is a celebration of African knowledge. Humankind emerged in Africa, and with humans came stories as a means for sharing knowledge between people, through the generations. The rich and vibrant storytelling tradition of Africa is reflected in the visually exciting and compelling narratives of Story Press Africa's books, linking us all to our earliest roots and to one another. Discover the stories which are part of all of our stories. Story Press Africa: African knowledge. African Stories. Worldwide.

Story Press Africa is distributed in the US by Consortium and in Southern Africa by Lapa Uitgewers - lapa@lapa.co.za

Storymoja

Physical address	Njamba House
	Shanzu Road off Lower Kabete Road
	Nairobi
Postal Address	PO Box 264 – 00606
	Sarit Centre
	Nairobi
Website	www.storymojaafrica.co.ke
Email	info@storymojaafrica.co.ke
Phones	+254 772413323, +254 20 2089595, +254 728 285021, +254 733 838161
Facebook	Storymojaafrica
Twitter	Storymoja
Contacts	Abijah Keru

Storymoja was formed by writers who are committed to publishing contemporary East African writing of world-class standards. To date, Storymoja has published over seventy children's books. The motto is to get a book in every hand.

StoryTime

Website	storytime-african-publisher.blogspot.com
Email	storytime.publishing@gmail.com
Contacts	Ivor W. Hartmann

StoryTime is a micro African press dedicated to publishing short fiction by emerging and established African writers. We publish two serial anthologies: *African Roar* and *AfroSF*.

WEB DEVELOPMENT   GRAPHIC DESIGN   ILLUSTRATION

DESIGNS

With over 20 years' experience, we specialise in websites for publishers, authors, artists and NPOs.

Designed for mobile

Easy to update

Training provided

www.tntdesigns.co.za

Techmate Publishers Ltd

Postal Address	PO Box 6667
	Accra North
Email	techmatepublishers@gmail.com
Phone	+233 24 426 2098
Contacts	Heena Karamchandani

GHANA

Our aim is to publish local authors' work so their works are made available to the general public and at a moderate price. We are also working on developing children's books.

uHlanga

Physical address	Cape Town
Website	www.uhlangapress.co.za
Email	editorial@uhlangapress.co.za
Phone	+27 83 645 1412
Twitter	uHlangaPress
Contacts	Nick Mulgrew

Founded in 2014, uHlanga is South Africa's progressive poetry press. The publisher of Koleka Putuma, Thabo Jijana, Saaleha Idrees Bamjee, Francine Simon and many others, uHlanga foregrounds the urgent, the experimental, the beautiful, and – most importantly – the enjoyable.

uHlanga's books have been bestsellers, named Book of the Year by City Press, and have won or been commended for the Ingrid Jonker Prize, the South African Literary Award for Poetry and the Glenna Luschei Prize for African Poetry.

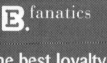

University of Namibia Press

Postal Address	Private Bag 13301
	340 Mandume Ndemufayo Ave
	Pionierspark
	Windhoek
Website	www.unam.edu.na/unam-press
Email	unampress@unam.na
Phone	+264 61 206 4714
Contacts	Dr Jill Kinahan

UNAM Press publishes works on topics related to Namibia and the Southern African region. Published and forthcoming titles include studies of literature, language and culture; education and democracy; statutory and customary law; public policy; social and political history; autobiographies; and indigenous knowledge.

Weaver Press

Physical address	38 Broadlands Road
	Emerald Hill
	Harare
Postal Address	P.O. Box A1922
	Avondale
	Harare
Website	www.weaverpresszimbabwe.com
Email	weaveradmin@mango.zw
Phone	+263 4 308330
Contacts	Njabulo Mbono

Weaver Press is a small publishing house committed to the production and distribution of the best of Zimbabwe's creative writing and scholarly research. It was established in 1998, since when it has developed a solid reputation for excellent editorial and production standards. As well as publishing contemporary fiction, we work with researchers and academic authors to produce books which reflect the developing tensions, challenges and prospects for Zimbabwean society; we also, on occasion, undertake freelance editing and typesetting.

Articles

Publishing the Indie Way
An interview with Joanne Macgregor

COLLEEN HIGGS

1. Why did you decide to go the self-publishing route?

I had a very good experience with traditional publishing - my publishers were professional, my editor was fabulous, and I had lots of input into the whole process. I've had four books traditionally published (five if you count a translation), but it soon became clear to me that the reading market in South Africa is very small, especially if you're not writing books for the textbook market. It made no sense to me to spend years writing a book and then personally do a lot of marketing and promotion, only to wind up selling one to two thousand copies. While those are perfectly respectable sales numbers, the small percentage of royalties earned was never going to be enough to provide a living for me, which is one of my writing goals. I also wanted to get more marketing than the publisher could provide, and wanted to be able to bring out more than one title a year (which was their policy).

I'd had a great idea for a book fall into my head, and I decided to set the story in the USA and see if I could break into that massive market. Initially, I went the traditional route - the protracted and agonising process of trying to land an agent and then submitting to publishers. I signed with an agent and was disappointed when she wasn't able to place the manuscript with a good publisher. By then I was so invested in that book (*Scarred*, a young adult contemporary romance) and had done so many rewrites, that I was determined to bring it to market, so at the end of 2015 I decided to self-publish it as an experiment. Luckily (and for no real reason that I can identify now that I know the business better), it did well - easily earning more than all my traditional titles combined. Self-publishing also allowed me total control and flexibility, speed to market, plus the marketing that I did resulted in increased pay directly to me, rather than to publishers or book stores. I was hooked!

Now I have twelve indie titles out (including boxed sets) and last year was granted a reversion of digital rights from my publishers, so I'm starting to bring those titles out, too. I have no beef with traditional publishing, but it would need to be a very good deal to tempt me back into that stable.

I do, however, still have one foot in the trad world. Last year I signed with an agent who specializes in international rights and have since had one of my titles (*The Law of Tall Girls*) translated into Polish, where it's sold so well that I've been approached on two more books for that market. That agent also negotiated the sale of the audio rights of *The law of Tall Girls to* Tantor Media, who brought the audiobook out this year. One of the perks of publishing independently is that you can sell your rights to publish in different languages and media in this way, and so create multiple streams of income. Too often, authors sign away all their rights in traditional contracts with publishers who have no intention, or even ability, to pursue subsidiary rights.

2. How long have you been publishing?

My first book, *Turtle Walk* (traditionally published) came out in 2011, and I've published every year since then.

3. You are known as an example of someone who has made a success of self-publishing - can you tell us what you think you have done right?

I made a lot of mistakes, but I did get a couple of things right, even if some of those were only accidental!

I know some folk in South Africa might not approve, but I think setting most of my books in the USA made it easier for readers there to take a chance on me. While I was still on the submissions and rewrites carousel of hell, I read a piece of advice to keep writing and I'm so glad I did, because by the time I decided indie was the way for me, I already had a few manuscripts and outlines written, so I was able to release those relatively quickly - which definitely helps with building a readership in the publishing world. For example, I was able to bring all three books in my Recoil Trilogy (YA dystopian) out in 2016, at three-month intervals. This meant that I could have the next book in the series already up on Amazon and available for preorder by the time the previous book was published, and could include a buy link in the back matter of the book. One of my best moves was to start thinking of myself as an author-entrepreneur. If you're going to go the indie route, you need to be prepared to market, sell, hustle and promote yourself. If you're wedded to the idea of the writer as a "pure" artiste unsullied by the taint of commerce, then you're very unlikely to succeed in the indie world.

Right from the get go, I decided that I wanted my indie titles to be as good or better than my traditionally published titles, so I've invested time (plus blood, sweat and tears) in writing the best books I could, plus I've invested good money in editors, proofreaders, professional formatters and wonderful covers. I think this is one of the reasons why they still sell, even years after publication.

4. Do you face any stumbling blocks in the SA book trade? Have you been able to overcome these?

On the traditional side, it can be difficult to get your book published, especially if you're not a well-known figure and your book is fiction and pure, escapist entertainment. I think publishers (everywhere, not just in SA) have very limited marketing budgets and resources, and these are often focussed on a few big name titles (usually international bestsellers), which means that new or midlist authors get to suck hind teat. When their titles don't take off, the idea that local books don't sell is reinforced and publishers are even more reluctant to take a chance on someone, or something, new.

On the indie side, the community of self-published writers in SA is small, but happily it's growing and seems to be following the same mutually-supportive path as tends to be the rule internationally. Our biggest problem is the distribution of paperbacks in South and southern Africa. We typically cannot go directly to the major book stores, and using intermediary vendors is so prohibitively expensive that we earn cents on the sale of paperbacks this way, while shouldering all the risk of sale-or-return policies. I, like many (if not most) local indies, sell directly off my website and don't bother with the big stores. In any event, our sales tend to be primarily in the ebooks market which, despite what you may have read, is thriving. I think I earn at least 95% of my royalties from digital income.

I guess the biggest challenge to writers of all kinds in South Africa is that our market of people who buy books isn't nearly as big as we want it to be. I'm very encouraged, however, to see this is changing and l look forward to the day when we're truly a reading nation.

5. Do you have advice for people who might want to go your route - a few dos and don'ts?

Define what "success" means to you. If you want a shot at prestigious literary awards, inclusion in and respect from the traditional publishing world, public acclaim, reviews in newspapers and magazines, to spend the bulk of your time in writing, and if you hate selling, then you should probably try your luck in traditional publishing. (This is doubly true if you write in the literary fiction or children's fiction genres, as those aren't big sellers in the indie and digital worlds.)

If, on the other hand, you write in genres that sell well (romance, crime and thrillers, fantasy, etc.), if your goal is to make a decent living off your writing (rather than to win kudos and literary accolades), if you're prepared to get out there and do what it takes to sell, and if you are not afraid of working harder than you ever have in your life - give self-publishing a shot!

Do find your tribe. Writing, especially as an indie, can be an isolated experience. There are wonderful groups of writers and indie-authors on Facebook - just search for your genre and jump in. You'll find they're a terrific source of advice, support and encouragement.

Do write the best quality book you can, and give it the best cover you can afford. Once it's published, it's up forever. Make sure you're proud of your work. Don't rush to market with an inferior product - I promise that (sadly) there aren't hordes of eager readers out there just waiting to buy your books. The world won't end if you take another six months or a year to get a good edit, do another rewrite, commission a better cover.

Do read as much as you can, especially in the genre in which you write. You are, of course, free to write what you like, but if you ever want to sell your books, they do need to fit into known genres.

Do sign up for podcasts on writing and self-publishing. Honestly, these are a fantastic resource - I often joke that everything I know, I learned on podcasts. I suggest starting with The Creative Penn podcast, The Career Author, The Sell More Books podcast, The Self-Publishing Formula, and the Science Fiction and Fantasy Marketing podcast.

Oh, and for the love of all that's holy, don't design your own covers!

So what if it is a good book?
and other lessons I am learning about publishing

NYANA KAKOMA

It was Nigerian poet Ijeoma Umebinyuo who told us to start. To start where we are. To start with fear. To start with pain. To start with doubt. To start with our hands shaking, voices trembling. To just start.

And so I did in June 2016 when Sooo Many Stories, published it's first title, a poetry collection by Ugandan poet, Peter Kagayi. When I look back now, I feel like I was well equipped with everything Ijeoma says to start with. There were innumerable things I was uncertain of and only one I knew for sure; that Peter Kagayi had some things to say, things that I believed needed to be said.

But there are things even a world-class editing class and a remarkable publishing internship in one of the best publishing houses you know, can never prepare you for. Things you will only learn just because you started.

So what if it is a good book?

This is a lesson I learnt really fast. It is not enough to have a well-written, perfectly edited and beautifully laid-out book. It is even worse if it is in a country where you are often reminded of the poor reading culture whenever you say the word "reading", and even worse when it is poetry. The fact that it could be the best poetry ever written is not enough. This has taught me to think about what the book looks like, how it can be creatively marketed, and how to creatively make sure it gets to people as easily as possible. This has stretched the way I look at manuscripts, how books are introduced to the public and how to think outside the box when it comes to books. It has changed the way I look at people who do not have any interest in books; to look at them as people I can interest, people I can convert and tuck away that snobbishness us book enthusiasts reserve for people that do not share this precious interest we have. It has pushed me out of my shell into interesting collaborations and spaces that I would never have been caught dead in before.

Ask, and you shall receive.

This is a lesson I am still learning. So you open this publishing house and you are the publishing director, HR Manager, Marketing Executive, Sales Executive, Public Relations person, Events coordinator, events decorator, finance chick, book distributor, and inevitably, the tea girl. Very soon you realise you can't do everything (your body won't let you hear the end of it and your brain starts to drop a few balls here and there).

I have been shocked by the kind of help I have received from strangers and friends alike, most times without my asking (because I did not know I needed it or was too scared to ask). From my brother, who at the launch of *The Headline That Morning* pulled me aside and said he was hesitant to buy a poetry book (poetry is not his kind of thing) but instead gave me money to "open a bank account, register with the revenue authority, you know…formalise your business". Help came from a stranger (now a dear friend), the second person to order for a copy of *The*

Headline That Morning and the very person who sent me a message the morning of the launch to encourage, affirm and celebrate my efforts. Help came when a Kenyan Blogger friend took the bus from Nairobi to Kampala, at his own cost, to be there for the launch of *The Headline That Morning*. Help came when a friend, who could not make it for the launch, offered to come and get the venue ready for the launch of the East African edition of *Flame and Song* by Philippa Namutebi Kabali-Kagwa, our second title. Help came when a young lady attended our adults' book club and after, she called to offer her time because she believed in what we are doing. I had no money to pay someone to do our social media work and yet, it was increasingly becoming too much for me to handle with the rest of the work I had to do.

Help still pours in from friends in the publishing world, visionary women that have gone ahead of me and made it much easier for me to live this dream; Bibi Bakare-Yusuf and Colleen Higgs continue to advise and make it all easier. Help still pours in from volunteers who set aside time every month to make reading fun for our children in our monthly book club.

Help pours in in ways too many to mention. Helps pours in from people who ask that you never publicly talk about how much they have supported you; they are just doing it because they believe in what you do. Help comes. Ask and you shall receive.

You don't have to fix all the problems today.

Another lesson I am still learning. You will not fix how the book shops look at local writers and how the government looks at the arts and how writers look at publishers and how people perceive books and how stories are told and what your family thinks of your work and how other people in the industry look at you TODAY! You don't have to know all the publishing models today. You do not have to have read all the bestsellers on all the bestselling lists. You can say no to manuscripts and you will not be guilty of crippling the publishing industry. You do not have to know everything and fix everything.

When in doubt, look to the children.

This is perhaps the main reason I have not thrown in the towel yet. We started Fireplaces (book clubs) for children, teenagers and adults shortly after we had launched our first book. The Children's Fireplace is a constant reminder of the importance of our work and the need for us to do more. We have received feedback from parents about the change in their children since they started attending the book club. And it has been change as significant as winning spelling and vocabulary contests and change as mind-blowing as a six year old attempting to retell the story she was told at the book club to her neighbourhood friends. It's seeing children's confidence grow as they read aloud to other members of the Fireplace or parents telling us that the children have been asking when the next book club is.

From the book club, we got requests to train young writers and we had our first children's writing workshop in December last year. We will be publishing an anthology from that workshop this year and we can't wait to see good books with faces they can relate to in book shops and school libraries in Uganda.

I look to the children to see the bigger picture of this often frustrating work and to be reminded why I started.

Why should we publish our work?

DAWN GARISCH, CEO: LIFE RIGHTING COLLECTIVE

Just over a year ago, a group of writers helped me to raise funds to form the Life Righting Collective. The main aim was to assist disadvantaged writers. We felt strongly that we should also publish an anthology of life writing, despite the time and effort involved in a market where it is difficult to see books. Why?

The unsustainability of perpetual busyness

I am also a medical doctor. It strikes me how stressed and overworked many patients are. We have created a society that is often too busy and exhausted to participate in creative and civic life, and to be self-reflective. This perpetuates a system that is unsustainable and does significant damage to individuals, communities and the earth.

Where do we go for pleasure?

I sometimes ask patients on the verge of burn-out: what do you do for pleasure? Mostly they stare at me, astonished, then they might offer something like watching movies or going to the gym. When pressed, they might admit that they used to play a musical instrument or write poetry. They took pottery or dance classes. Then life became too demanding and the creative pursuit had to go because it was a 'hobby' that didn't pay.

We have abdicated our creativity and handed it over to professionals.

True creativity is messy

Creative engagement is a birthright. Jaak Panksepp, the Nobel-winning neuroscientist, has described how humans are born with an innate capacity for play. We cannot learn how to play because we need to play in order to learn. To play is to experiment, taking risks without knowing what is going to happen next. It is fuelled by curiosity and excitement. It feeds on paradox, contradiction and strange juxtapositions that open up new and surprising possibilities.

Creativity gets us out of the box of logic and reasoning – tools that are necessary but that are overvalued in our culture. From the time we are small, we are schooled to believe there is only one answer and you had better know it. We become afraid to experiment in case we look silly, or make a mess, or don't produce a masterpiece first time round.

Reclaim your curiosity

So, the first half of this article is a call for us to reclaim our inborn creativity as a valuable tool. We need to become curious about ourselves, our communities and the world. Creative writing is one way to discover what we don't know we don't know.

Our unconscious patterns and habits, as well as the images and emotions that shape our lives, can become clearer to us when we have a conversation with ourselves on the page. We can improve awareness and observation about our habits and tendencies and how we impact on each other and the earth. We can grow compassion and act more kindly. I think of creative writing as an act of mental health. Our mental health affects our physical health. This has value that no money can buy.

What has this to do with publishing our stories?

So why publish? When I first started teaching life writing eight years ago, I purposefully downplayed the aspect of getting published, because if you have one eye on the market and another on the cash register, you will never do your best work. However, I have seen how the act of reading one's work to others during a life writing course can grow confidence and kindness in the reader/writer, and how hearing another person's story can help the listener to revisit their assumptions. By relating our lives to each other, we become more related.

This is why!

Initially I felt ambivalent about the much bigger step of bringing writers' work into the world. I have always emphasised that our creativity is about growing community rather than a hierarchy of who writes better than whom. Getting into the download space requires us to set aside judgement and to make ourselves available to whatever needs to be written.

I have seen too many writers stop writing if their work was judged not good enough to make it into print. But so much excellent writing was coming out of the writing courses that would never get published by mainstream publishing houses that I felt sad. Not only was the writing worth reading for its own sake, but the stories were having an impact on those who heard them. Our society is traumatised and we need avenues to help connect us as human beings after decades of institutionalised prejudice and separation.

So when we raised funds for the first year of operation of Life Righting Collective, we included a budget for publishing a first anthology of life writing, advertised in this catalogue on page 58, and for creating a website to post more true stories written by South Africans from all walks of life.

The collection in our anthology *This Is How It Is* is tender, moving, hilarious, disturbing, quirky and surprising. There are stories written by seasoned writers and beginners. They all reflect our shared humanity in courageous ways.

Reading them has opened my heart.

This is how it is is available in all good bookshops and from www.jacana.co.za.

Dawn Garisch is a medical doctor, author, poet and CEO of the Life Righting Collective: www.liferighting.com

Publishing and Money

COLLEEN HIGGS

There is the old joke "How do you make a small fortune from publishing?" "You start with a large one." But what if you had no fortune to start with? Just a small pension and an ability to compartmentalize and the crazy unbridled optimism of someone who learns from her mistakes, usually, and who nevertheless in spite of more setbacks than she can begin to count is still irrepressibly optimistic. I keep thinking it is getting better. And it is. But is it really?

Money has been at the heart of my work as a publisher. Not enough money. Not ever. But somehow I'm still here eleven years later. Nothing is certain. Nothing is guaranteed, even for those who have financial reserves, which I don't. However, coming clean about the money side of how I've operated as a small independent publisher feels important, even if it feels more shameful than talking about some sexual fetish or predilection I might have.

I've come to realise why most small, independent, literary publishers in the world are attached to larger institutions or are non-profits or have other jobs, and do their publishing as a small part of what they do. For some reason when I started Modjaji I decided to try and make it work as a business.

I often feel weighed down by the financial debt that publishing has brought with it, I feel weighed down by the guilt of all those I owe money to. The anxiety is an ever-present, unwelcome companion that I have learnt to live with. The worrying about money is a bit like bobbing on a lilo. The day-to-day survival mode makes it difficult to dive deep and to think of larger, more long lasting solutions and strategies. I live day-to-day, hand to mouth. And yet I manage. Money flows in. Money flows out.

At times I do feel ashamed of how I have no money. My credit card is maxed out. I owe writers royalties. I've been lucky enough to get to the Frankfurt Book Fair every year since 2011, with funding. But I've been to Frankfurt with almost no money. But there are lots of drinks parties with snacks, often there has been a breakfast thrown in with the accommodation funding from the Department of Trade and Industry.

Every month as I pay the bond on my house and my daughter's school fees it feels like a triumph, an achievement. But then I have to do it again the next month and the one after that. But I try not to dwell on it. Each month is a series of hurdles of bills to pay. Most days my bank account is debited. Bond, bank charges, interest, credit card payments, medical aid, house insurance, car insurance, life insurance. Telkom, Vodacom and then Afrihost for the website and ADSL and data, Google each month and once a year Dropbox. Often I'm surprised and dismayed when money I thought was there is no longer. My money ride is a lurching, jarring ride. At times I long for a smoother ride, one that is less frightening.

Publishing is a cost-intensive business. I have to pay manuscript readers, editors, proofreaders, book designers, cover artists, illustrators, printers (theirs are the biggest bills), PR costs, couriers (a big part of publishing – getting books delivered), launch costs.

Over the years I have developed additional income streams for Modjaji Books. There are rights sales, permissions, and direct sales to authors, pop-up book sales. I've given seminars on publishing. I've read manuscripts for a fee. I've advised individuals about their publishing projects for a fee, I see this work as writing and publishing therapy. I create Special Offers on Facebook. Small subsidies have come from some writers who work at universities and who can access money from their research accounts to make a subvention payment towards their books. I've received a small amount of funding from a couple of funding agencies in South Africa, but never from the National Arts Council. I have now given up applying to them. In addition I have sold shares in the company to friends who also believe in the value of publishing southern African women writers.

Modjaji has also had some extraordinarily generous donations from kind benefactors for particular titles and once a writer kindly donated an airfare to Frankfurt in a year when the DTI funding didn't come through. I've tried crowd funding for one book – the beautiful *A to Z of Amazing South African Women*, published last year and successfully raised R100,000. It might sound a lot but producing a full colour litho-printed book is costly.

Generous friends and family and some writers have loaned me money interest free. Some service providers have donated their work. All of these things have kept Modjaji Books afloat. I have learnt how to accept generosity from others and I've learnt humility and gratitude.

I've also made some tough decisions – for example I decided that Modjaji wouldn't pay poets royalties. They get a generous discount on books that they can sell and are encouraged to sell books themselves at readings and to their own networks. But any money that Modjaji makes from poetry goes into the Poetry Fund to make it possible to publish other poets. It is not easy to break even publishing poetry.

Independent publishing without a large fortune is a nerve wracking, anxiety filled enterprise. It's not for the fainthearted. But the non-financial rewards are immeasurable. More about that next time.

First published on the Nigerian online magazine, Book Republic
(https://bookrepublic.com.ng/2018/06/11/publishing-and-money-1-colleen-higgs/)

Weaver Press – a short history

MURRAY MCCARTNEY AND IRENE STAUNTON

Weaver Press is a limited liability company (No. 5188/98) registered in Zimbabwe in 1998.

In spite of its formal status, Weaver operates more like a non-profit, or NGO. It is run by two owner-directors, Irene Staunton and Murray McCartney, together with a publishing assistant, Njabulo Mbono, and operates from a home office on the owners' property.

Our founding principal was to ensure that the results of Zimbabwean creative writing and scholarship be made available in their country of origin, rather than being published exclusively abroad, as had often been the case in the past. This has involved co-publishing arrangements with academic presses in the UK and USA, and partnership with donor agencies and foundations; examples of the latter include Hivos, Ford Foundation, Rockefeller Foundation, Friedrich Ebert Stiftung, Konrad Adenauer Stiftung and the British Council.

Over the twenty years of it existence, Weaver Press it has earned a reputation as the country's foremost publisher of fiction, academic non-fiction and political biography. In the early days, we assumed that financial self-sufficiency would be achieved in a matter of years; however, and particularly during the past decade, the national economic environment has been inhospitable: inflation has had a dramatic impact on both our costs and our customers, and book sales are now generally modest; for titles prescribed on school syllabi, sales are affected by rampant piracy. And yet the need for independent publishing remains as urgent as ever, in terms of both creative writing and serious scholarship.

Much has been written about – and many reasons have been given for – the lack of a 'reading culture' in Zimbabwe. Fingers have been pointed at the rise of social media, the decline in educational standards, and the decaying state of public libraries, but little has been said about the paucity of appropriate books. These don't necessarily have to be by Zimbabweans or about Zimbabwe – the success here of Chimamande Adichie's *Purple Hibiscus* is evidence that a good story can cross national boundaries with ease – but there's no doubt that people can relate more easily to, and be drawn in by, writing that acknowledges their culture and circumstances.

In the years since Weaver Press was founded, other general publishers and local university presses have more or less ceased operating; only school textbook publishers remain. Weaver itself has only survived through a combination of low overheads, modest salaries, and a fervent commitment to the work.

However, the school market remains crucial to our survival, and accounts for some 80% of our sales. We have never set out to publish books aimed specifically at this market; what we have done, is choose from our fiction list those titles that we regard as appropriate, and submit them for consideration to the local exams council for presciption in O and A Level syllabi.

Foreign markets represent a serious challenge for African publishers. There are many barriers – both formal and informal – to trade within the continent, and selling rights is nearly always better than trying to shift physical books from place to place. European and American markets are, ironically, more accessible, and membership of the Oxford-based African Books Collective is an essential part of our marketing strategy.

Beyond the range of our own publications, we do a considerable amount of freelance work for NGOs and development agencies. This usually involves editing, typesetting and liaising with designer and printers.

Publishing in African is certainly getting harder, rather than easier, but the rewards for perseverence remain enormous.

Why we started impepho press

impepho press is a Pan Africanist publishing house committed to the sincere telling of African and international stories, celebrating both the fragility and resilience of the human experience. We believe in championing brave, particularly feminist, voices committed to literary excellence.

Impepho, a species of wild chamomile, is a plant that can be used as incense and as a calmative. It can be used to meditate, to pray, to sooth anxiety, or to relieve a headache. Whether you burn it, boil it or soak in it, it has a way of calming what is restless and unlocking what is blocked.

Sometime around 1989, Tanya Pretorius picked up *Geek Love* by Kathrine Dunn, a book that taught her about "the value of being unique, and family. Community. Real, not homogenous peer-induced ankle-crossing ignorance." At twelve years old, Sarah Godsell picked up her first copy of *The Little Prince* by Antoine de Saint-Exupéry. It taught her about love, loneliness, friendship and care. Most importantly, it taught her about hope and empathy. "How to have and find home for something, somewhere." For me it was *I Know Why the Caged Bird Sings* by Maya Angelou. I had just finished grade eleven and was suffering from severe depression. I had grown quiet, no longer questioning. And here was a little girl who had lost, then found her voice again. Angelou taught me to live. To breathe. To not die. And I have been living ever since.

For all three of us, books have saved our lives. Have taught us to be better versions of ourselves. And this is how we came together. We wanted to create a company that is hearted by healing. We wanted to read books that tell human stories, pretty and ugly, with sincerity and skill. So we decided to write them. And if we could not write them ourselves, we would find them, and we would publish them.

We also wanted to affect representation. One cannot deny that South Africa still faces many challenges, particularly around race, class and gender. These challenges, inevitably, spill into the publishing sector, and therefore feed back into society. When one looks at the books being sold in major books stores, and the books available in community libraries, one can see very clearly that real transformation is *not yet uhuru*. The "African Literature" section reflects access, more than the existence of stories. Authors are not known as authors in their home towns because libraries and small book shops do not have their books. Or authors cannot get beyond their small communities, no matter how good their books are, because they don't have access to avenues of distribution. And books are expensive… therefore books are a luxury.

Kim Addonizzio and Dorrainne Laux (*The Poet's Companion: A Guide to the Pleasures of Writing*) wrote: "Writing a poem in such times may feel like fiddling while Rome burns. Yet we're poets. Writing is what we do in the world – or part of it anyway – and as ephemeral as it might sometimes seem, the making of poems is a necessary act, one that allies itself with hope rather than despair."

impepho press wants to ally itself with hope. And beyond being writers, we have an opportunity to publish stories that may not otherwise have been published. As **impepho press**, we want black girls to experience a multitude of black girl stories and know they are not a monolith. We want readers to see that Africa is filled with colours, and that there is a whole world of Angela Carter *Wayward Girls and Wicked Women* for them to explore. We want to get those books on people's bookshelves. In their bags, next to their beds, on their toilet tops. We want to small community libraries and book shops to have our books, and we want big chain stores to stock our books.

We want to make the less visible, visible!

Poetry will always be our first love. That being said, we are also very interested in short stories and creative non-fiction. As we grow, we hope to publish in various languages, and to increase our genre portfolio, but one step at a time. For now, **impepho press** prides itself on striving to provide our authors with the best editorial, design and promotional support as possible, irrespective of the stages in their careers. At **impepho press**, we serve the stories, always! Because without our stories, we would, in the words of Audre Lorde, be crumpled into other people's fantasies of us and eaten alive.

Printed in the United States
By Bookmasters